ALSO, BY KASHYA MOLINEAUX

POETIC LITERATURE

Moods of The Soul

Lucid Thoughts of The Soul

Perspectives of Experience

Whispers of Purpose

CHILDREN LITERATURE

Amari's Imagination Day

Amari Learns the Gift of Giving

Kashya Molineaux

I KNOW WHY BLACK GIRLS CRY

Dedicated to all the Black Women, who yearn to be understood, while accountability is present.

Dedicated to Marjorie Phillips.

I know you're watching over me.

Introduction

I Know Why Black Girls Cry, is a poetic novel that dives deep into the traumas that many young black women face. I, being a black woman in America, can correlate my experience as the feeling of being in a haunted house. In this haunted house there are forces aimed at intimidating you. To steal your voice and dim your soul. It's as if everyone in this house seeks torment, until you respond how they feel you should react. Though in reality you are the center of attention, with a powerful voice, that cannot be silenced. Often, particularly Black Women are criticized in society, and labeled by terms deemed to portray them in a demeaning way. Today, there are multiple voices screaming, as to what a Black woman should be like. However, there are hardly any voices exclaiming, as to how society has helped to scar the mentality of many black women. From the beginning of slavery to the damaged mentalities and concept of the Black family structure. Being a Black Woman in America, is to be misunderstood, judged, and classified as a whole, rather than your own unique individuality. I Know Why Black Girls Cry, goes in depth to further evaluate the scarring tears, that many black women hide, as their sanity mirrors the misunderstood aspect that lay beyond the surface of a Black Woman in America. This novel is aimed to unmask the haunting pain, that haunt many black women. All Black Women simply deserve the mental clarity and freedom of being heard and understood.

Chapter 1
Tears Felt

Tears Go

Where do the tears go …
That travel on roads alone …
I want to know
Where do my tears go
As they stream down my face
Do they dry up and find a new journey to embrace …
Or do they vanish due to the fear of never healing …
Each tear released from my eye
Is the releasing of vulnerability and pride
It all started that night …
When my words were no longer
Heard within your ears …
When my eyes, became completely white
My pupils were no longer present in your vision …
You couldn't see me,
Hell, you couldn't even see yourself
Instead of hearing and seeing me …
You whipped me, with every bashful expression
All for me to assume, I was less than
You told me "I wasn't beautiful "
So, my confidence of beauty faded
I became the coldest and ugliest version of me
After all, I was now the curse of your screams
So unaware …
I was beautiful
But that lacking in you, decided I needed to hurt too
Fortunately for me, I am worth love
No matter how many times, you scolded me with hate
You became your own enemy
Backfiring, for me to be great
I once listened to you
And your traumatizing demons …
I was there …I heard you at night screaming
It was clear you needed help…

Though you stopped believing …
You let hurt take over and lost your sanity
You felt alone …
Yearning for your insane, to take over my brain
Though I wasn't born weak,
I pushed your words aside
Began to hold my head high
Indeed …
I am the pride
Of every conquered battled
Inside

The Understanding

It is true… hurt people. People's actions reflect their inner selves. If someone is truly happy with who they are, they are most likely to spread inner joy within themselves, because they are not of pain. Those who have unresolved self-issues can become enemies of themselves. Therefore, do not expect those who treat themselves badly to treat you with goodness and grace, as you deserve.

When someone becomes their enemy of themselves, their viewing of the world projects a negative attitude towards life. Becoming an enemy to yourself not only harms you, but affects those around you, who care. You reflect, everything you believe to be true, and every thought you embrace as you. Be wary of those who aren't kind to themselves and aren't appreciative of the love they have surrounding them. Understand, it is not up to you to become their savior. It is only up to you to know who and what you deserve.

Whether it be a family member, significant other, or a friend, it is crucial to ensure that you are being respected on or beyond the level of respect that you give. Never make excuses for someone's discourteous actions towards you. Remember that your emotional intelligence will affect many factors in your life. Instead of reflecting someone's negative energy towards you, become better. Show them and yourselves, that no matter what comes your way, you cannot be broken. Believe that you are better than what you've been through. Your hardest days should never conquer you. You conquer them. Always.

Worth More
At an early age
You were introduced to the idea of
"In the sheets"
In the sheets you did not make choices
And there was no escape
You numbed the feeling "in the sheets"
Knowing the act was not meant to be
Soon, you began to control and say no
You thought you escaped …
You thought you ran fast enough …
But then…you lay down with a guy of choice
He gives you a warm heart
He has the sparkle in his eyes …
He's the first …you choose between your thighs
Then he enters you within …
Suddenly he feels like sin
He reopens wounds, that were covered in a temporary bandage
You resort to what you know …
You numb yourself, and you can't feel him
Your mind fills with anger
Hot tears stream down your face
As it now feels you are with a stranger …
Though in truth
The stranger is you ...
Each stroke you've ever felt
Was the entering of confusion
You are confused, because you have been abused
Unconsciously you'll search for someone like you
Hoping they feel what you feel, and you'll mistake this as real
It is the bond of trauma, that will release your inner drama
You'll realize, you don't need sex

You need your self
To become your self
Give yourself the help …
To learn who you are
To see your true beauty inside
Though it is your decision to decide …
Despite what you've been through
You need to know you are worth so much more ...

The Understanding

Sexual abuse is not only physical. Sexual abuse is damaging to the heart, mentality, and self. Those who have suffered sexual abuse may find it hard to connect with themselves and others. It becomes impossible to feel that you are enough, or even simply to feel. To feel and know what is real, and to feel that you are valuable beyond sex. Like any human, you want the feelings that sex can bring. Relaxation, connection, and trust.

However, when you have been taken advantage of, sex becomes your enemy. Sex can become the reminiscing of pain; you thought you tamed. It can be the releasing of deep emotions, you've held within. The memories of a sexual abuse experience can feel intense. It can feel like a roaring tiger chasing you. With every step you take, even in the deepest of your dreams, it seems to always be there.

For the painful experiences that you've endured. It is important to understand that running away from your fears, and thoughts, will never save you. If you are always running from your enemy, then you will always be running. However, when you address and conquer the enemy, you become the resolution to your inner conflicts. Know that avoidance will not erase the pain. When you suppress emotions, the more pain will absorb within the roots of your heart. Learn yourself, learn your weaknesses, and know your strengths. Give yourself patience and grace, to know that you are worth every bit of help you give to yourself. There is nothing wrong with being ready, when you are ready.

If Friends

I wish…
That I could open my heart
So that towards friendships…
I would never feel apart
If my trust was as rich as the rivers of time…
Maybe I could be held, through unheard cries
Instead …
I drop tears alone
Sweeping vulnerability across the room
Praying for the healing and closing of wounds
Yearning for someone to run to…
When I'm not okay …
I wish I had a friend to say
It's okay …to have a bad day
Though I'll be with you
Every step of the way…
Like a true friend
Would likely say …

The Understanding

Trust plays a major role in allowing people to live within your life. However, with trust comes along, vulnerability. Vulnerability is the allowing of freedom within your emotions. If you've had negative experiences with those you have considered close friends, then you may find it hard to rebuild trust in others. Indeed, it is the protection of yourself, but the rejection of something else.

We all need love, rather it be romantic, or platonic. Past relationships with others cannot be the defining of your future relationships. Trust issues within yourself, and others, will isolate you from sharing memorable and meaningful experiences with those who truly value and adore you.

Know that there are genuine people in this world, just like there are those who aren't of good nature. However, it is not up to you to judge everyone based on your lack of trust. Trust that people will show you who they are, before placing a negative view upon them. Understand, that you call the shots in your life, realistically no one must be in your life, unless you allow them to be. Choose your company wisely, as your company can be the breaking or uplifting of you.

Where's My Hug?

I just wanted a hug …
A hug that felt like home
One that felt like true warmth and protection
A forehead kiss, to make me feel like a princess
Maybe a lecture …to tell me that I was perfect
I wanted congratulating tears to show me I was worth all the cheers …
I wanted, I yearned, I cried
For years and years …
Hoping one day you'd appear
But here comes mama …
She tells me you never cared
She tells me my birth was everything but pleasant to your ears …
Every night, I lay in bed
Wishing that I received more than just a mother's love
The kind of love, that "normal" kids felt
I craved the balance of a motherly and fatherly presence
Soon, I began to conclude that I was less than
If my father did not want me
For sure …I believed a stranger could never love me
I lost my heart in the bitterness of your nonexistence
I drank with the mentality of drowning you from my imaginative reality
I smoked, and became high

Praying …that at heart you were a much better guy
Though soon, my heart flooded with "Daddy issues "
My ears were covered in confusion
And every man, that spoke to me
Labeled me angry, in conclusion
It's true …I was frustrated
Even more …hurt
Simply because…
I was your daughter
And your love me for me, should have come first

The Understanding

For the children, who grew up without a father…know that it is not your fault. Responsibility is a mentality that not everyone is able to accept. Lack of someone else's responsibility does not determine your value or worth. Realistically speaking, for most there will never be a suitable answer, as to why a father decided not to be in their child's life. Though whole fully aim to be better, than what you were given in this world, as an appreciation of your existence.

Before, reacting with anger, listen for the truth. Do not allow someone else's words to define your relationship with someone else. Be open to building a forward connection, with a past wound, to close this wound. Release your honest feelings, remember that your thoughts are valid. Where emptiness within you resides, reach out to gain a sense of fulfilment.

As above stated, you decide who chooses to be in your life. If you feel this is a connection of necessity, for you to move forward, then go for it, if the option is present. Know that forgiveness is the key to the next step. Acknowledge your feelings towards lack of this relationship, though avoid letting it define you. Know that you are more than the people who have disappointed you.

Perfect Match

They say she got daddy issues
And ain't nobody ever cared for her
Yeah…they say she been scarred at birth
Miss girl …let me show you some love
The older man said, as his eyes gave my skirt a tug …
I moved closer, maybe this was home
He lovingly caressed his fingers on my soft skin
Maybe this is love …
I feel his mind capturing my youth in slow motion
I felt hypnotized in the best way…
In all his meeting felt like the day I'd become a woman
See…it's how he cared for me
The safety he presented for me
"You do this for me, and I give you everything you ever need "
Oooh yes, I fell for the lust and lacking love within me
He took advantage of the father I never knew
He kissed my forehead, mocking unconditional love
But in my head …I was his princess
I didn't care if the world didn't accept it …
I opened my legs, to feel the maturity of sex
Unaware mentally I was not there yet …
He made me believe he cured every pain in me
But he reminded me …don't fall too deep
He says…
I ain't ya daddy, I'm just here because you asked me …
He revealed his truth
But did I ask him?
Was my essence of lacking nurture, so strong?
Did I lure him in?
Did I commit sin, to let an older guy in …?
I was confused, so I left old dude
And for sure with an attitude, he said fuck you too
I never turned back, but I looked for what I lacked
I wanted love, real sex

I searched until I could find the best
But I never could
Simply because I attached my pain with sex
I was craving love, but in truth
I was unattached
Indeed, I only attracted …
"My perfect Match"

The Understanding

Know that there are people who will pry, on what they believe to be your weakness. Be aware of those who leave you feeling empty, rather than fulfilled. In most cases, where you consistently feel drained, in someone's presence it can mean in some way they are taking advantage of you. Be careful, do not be seduced by words. Understand that genuine actions are the greatest acts of love.

Know that the presence you seek, in an impractical manner, is the lacking within self. What you lack can either be your enemy, or your eye opener to life. Whether it be a person or an emotion, everything is supported by an essence. In some cases, an essence is not always able to be duplicated. Though it is important that you find replacements that elevate you both spiritually and mentally.

Only invite into your life, what serves you good. If you seek love through sex, know that this mentality is the quickest way to disappointment. Love originates from the heart; it is something non-physical. Fulfill yourself by giving the love to yourself that you deserve. Do not expect someone to be your savior, when most are unable to save themselves.

Chapter 2
Tears Heard

Blunt Fire

She releases her gut feelings …
Into the blunt
She rolls up …
For every time she was misunderstood
For every moment,
Intense anger occurred
She lights the fire
Attempting to burn reality
And inhales the soothing of a calm mentality
She exhales the unwanted emotions
That she is unable to face
It is pain, that she wishes not to embrace
She wants to be happy
Free from the midst of inner depression
Each ash, is the representation of a traumatic past
Not caring if anyone understands …
She rolls, hoping that one day
Someone licks her wounds …
She seals the blunt …
Hoping to one day, feel enough
And deep down…
She doesn't feel normal
So, she searches for answers,
To silence the questions …
"Like why this happened…"
As her only faith becomes heaven
Yearning to heal …praying to feel
…An essence of relief
Instead of the occurrence of grief
Like every human being …
She just wants peace
Though her surroundings
Unlocks the presence of anxiety
Her head fills with the pressure of society

So, she rolls a blunt …
Because that blunt will never judge
It won't abuse her, and call it love
She relies on it, with trust
Inhale, exhale
Temporarily she prevails, above her reality of hell
High…above her true feelings inside
High…because she really wants to hide
So High…
But, hi, I see you
I hope you know you're seen
Your aura is as beautiful as a majestic dream
I hear your screams
I know you're tired, but I believe in you
Through all the bullshit
I hope you stay inspired
Darling, never let anyone blow out the inner fire…

The Understanding

Naturally, as humans one thing we all have in common is a deep desire for happiness. We all want to feel as if our life on this earth has a purpose and serves us in grace.

Know that even when you think you aren't seen, someone sees you. When you think you aren't heard, someone will hear you. Open yourself up to feel what you don't allow yourself to feel. Hear yourself, you owe it to you, to be vulnerable. Suppressed pain may blur from the mind, though it will linger in the heart and spirit.

Be conscious of the reasoning and mentality behind any action that you complete. Always remain in control of you and be honest to truths that aren't always easy to accept. Understand, the fire you have within is the strongest and most beautiful flame you will ever ignite.

Sometimes…a Mother Cries

To the young single woman …
Raising her child
I know you have moments …
When you don't feel proud
You have days when your tears speak out loud …
Moments when you ask yourself why
Days when you don't feel blessed
Hours when you just simply feel stressed …
You need an ear, that listens
A prayer that offers a hand
Someone who is there, to truly show they care
A world where there is more action to love, than to judge
You yearn for your baby, to never sense your unstable
Holding pillows to your trauma
So that your little one, never absorbs your inner drama …
But you are more than a mama…
You are a woman, working to be the best she can be
No matter what they see or what they believe …
You are someone, who is worth everything
A mother devoting her feminine power into another life …
You are a soul, working to feel whole
We get it …
Darling, you are not alone
I know that the world eyes can feel so cold
They judge you …as if they are above you
But you are great,
God gave you the strength, to not easily break
You are blessed …
You have given life to unconditional love
Darling, you have overcome obstacles
That most would have been afraid to have done …
A woman, a mother
You are heavenly
Kiss yourself, value yourself

You are the true beauty of nature
Nothing less…

The Understanding

Motherhood, in any situation, can be challenging. It is important to know, there is no such thing as being completely perfect as a mother. Your version of perfect, and your child's version of perfect are probably two different things. Most children will appreciate your presence. It is the time spent, the I love you's and the warm smiles given to their children, that will embrace their memories in love.

Be there for your child, so that they know the value of unconditional love. There will be hard times, though trust that you will not be given anything in life that you can't handle. I believe as women, we all are mentally stronger and in tune, more than we think. Truly, it is up to you to believe it.

Knowing in your heart that you're a good mother is sometimes the only validation you'll ever need. Considering, there is always room to grow, though understand that you are growing, just like your child is growing. Be confident in your motherhood, avoid allowing the negative to overpower your gifts in life.

Know that your self-identity, beyond being a mother, is as relevant as you make it to be. Having a child does not make you any less you, you are still you. Even more you have a beautiful creation that admires you for you. Yes, there's always more learning to do, though I guarantee you're a better mother than you give yourself credit for. Know that you're doing great.

Too Many Opinions
She said …
My skin is too light …

He said my skin was too dark
They all said my hair was too nappy
And then I hear …
Stop wearing weaves
They all shake their heads in shame and disbelief …
Then I scream …
Because I'm stuck in between
My only freedom is the expression of my dreams
I bleached my skin, attempting to erase draining mentality sins
Perming my hair to blend in with my traumas
Damaged …
It feels each voice of opinion
Is a suffocating snake …
Slowly hissing at me, as they wrap their insecurities
Around my temple of life
So, I asked them…
Is my long weave
Haunting you in your dreams?
Does my Afro, give you the jitters
Or …is it my light skin, that reminds you of a slave masters, sin?
Maybe, my dark skin that mirrors your lacking acceptance within
Does my self-expression disrupt your acceptance into heaven?
Though it my boldness of truth
My unfelt need to conform to society needs …
That must make you feel incomplete
I am not a poster board of what black should be
I am the representation of what I am meant to be
In the moment …
My skin, is beautiful
In the moment …
My desired hairstyle is beautiful
In the moment, and forever
I will be the choice of me, no matter who accepts my entirety
I am a woman, who chooses to be …

The Understanding

Being a Black Woman, in America, means that many will admire you, as well as attempt to define you on their terms. It's as if, no matter what hair, skin, or size, you are in…there will always be an opinion as to what works for you. If you are a Black woman who chooses to wear weave, you will be bashed. A Black Woman, that wears their natural hair…some will accept you; others will consider you unkept.

If you are a light skinned Black woman, sometimes you are considered not black enough. Being a dark-skinned woman, you can be considered "too black". It's as if everyone has an opinion on what a black woman should be like, and less of an opinion of how Black Women, should be treated with respect and appreciated as they are.

Understand when everyone has an opinion as to how you should be, the best thing to do is to be and do what works for you. Put yourself first, and understand the comfort you have within yourself, is the only opinion that will ever truly matter. Live your life, for yourself. Know that most will never be pleased, simply because some are displeased with themselves. Be the greatest version of yourself, by choosing to be yourself no matter what others believe.

Thin Line
I know it's the cruel obsession
That once caused the tears of my depression
You took my strength, my king
Whipped him until his power became unseen
In my eyes, you aimed to make him weak
Your hatred and insecurity, traumatized a cultures maturity
Daughter and mothers, bonded through traumatic waters
Rape, now flowed through the veins of so many sisters
Causing many to lose touch of their true worth
Years passed; you declared us all free
Only for the government to intervene
Selling a dream, that a man is a thing no Sista needs

Now the white man, is the man of a Black mothers' house
And now a Sista believes, she did it on her own
When in reality …a Black family is a royal home
You pry on my babies, teaching them it all began with slavery
And you'd fail them… if they'd mention,
The consciousness of other dimensions
No…you'd rather keep them complacent
Tell them their hair is too nappy
To be joyful, with pride, and be happy
Destroying an image
Because your lack of self-love, you chose to diminish
We all cry in vain sometimes
When the ego, is present overshadowing the light …
One day we'll all realize that there was never truly a fight
Only an admiration, dressed in hate
Though when uncovered …it's love
Because there's a thin line between love and hate …
It's an obsession, that caused others a story of depression
To see beyond it, is the human lesson and blessing

The Understanding

Throughout American history, there has been racial conflict. For most, many believe that racial tensions began during slavery. It is crucial to understand, that slavery is not the defining of those with African descent. However, slavery has caused separation, depression, and generational trauma. Slavery was the brainwashing and degrading of a culture, causing many to lose traditional ways, as well as true self worth and love within.

In modern times, as we learn to become our own freedom, it is important to understand the depth of hate. Hate can be defined as envy and admiration. Meaning, what you convince yourself that you dislike in another person, in truth you deeply admire. Be conscious of the mentality, that someone's actions towards you, are not the defining of you. During those times, when you are approached by someone who is not at peace, trust the peace within to overpower the reject in them. Perspective is the truth of the mentality. Believe that there is more love than hate.

Your Enemy

Where do you go
When the clouds turn into fire
And the sky is no longer higher
And feet no longer feel inspired
Do you look up …
And ask why
Or do you turn to mirrors
With a silent cry ?
When your heart metamorphose into blue ice
Do you believe , you were cursed twice
Numbed and afraid of love
Do you blame others , that you can't trust
Do you truly feel you are enough
Are you blessed in the moment ?
Your life ?
Do you feel your own it?
See, let's get deeper into the crevices
That you are afraid to seek …
It is time to challenge
The enemy …
Your reflection has become the stump in your projection
Self perspective has been neglected
From a blinded view …
You never know where or who to turn to
When all along …
The answer and problem …

Is you …
Only you are the unstoppable of your unstoppable

The Understanding

It is important to understand that the only person that could ever hold you back is you. It is possible to be your own enemy in life. Whenever you go against your morals or break promises to yourself, you are the enemy of yourself.

Never go against yourself. In life, you should always aspire to be on your side, put yourself first. You determine the defining of yourself, be the representation of the greatness within.

Make it a priority to be kind to yourself. Take time to learn yourself. Acknowledge the areas of growth within yourself and give yourself the patience to become better. Don't be afraid to step out of your comfort zone, to explore the whole of you. Challenge yourself, to allow yourself to succeed to greater lengths. Believe in yourself and be appreciative of the life that you were given. It is your duty to love yourself to the fullest.

Chapter 3

Tears Seen

In Place

I'd raise my voice in frustration
Veins filled with past traumatic emotions
I'd stand humbly, hoping you would bless Patience over me
Just to listen …
Instead, you believed it was me ….
In need of a lesson
And due to your lacking emotional intelligence…
You reacted physically, with no self-discipline
I embraced your weakness of anger
Indeed… I believed I earned it …
Because …
You were right, and I was wrong
And you love me, and I love you
So, we'll always get along
I trusted this was how a relationship should be
You know Sometimes …
A woman needed to be put in her place
Called out her name,
So that she's know how to act and maintain …
You were just teaching me how to behave
While I played the part as your abused slave
Tears rolling down my face …
Only brought you guilt, after your hardest hits
You'd hug me, reminding me you'd never do it again
Whispering in my ear

"You're beautiful, forgive me for my sins "
After all were human, no one is perfect outside or within
So, who I am to judge …
Shouldn't I leave that to God above?
But you repeatedly commit your habit
Consistently your lack of discipline, would stab me
Your abandonment of accountability
Fueled the pain of the inner me
My lack of self-esteem led to my own harm
Then one day…
The sun became the power of my enlightenment
Eyes wide, I am aware
I didn't deserve your embedded demons
Nor did I earn, the unleashing of your self-hatred
I was beautiful, not because of you
But beyond you, and what I've been through
I was unaware, that you were the tears in my heart
That you were the distance of my soul and body growing apart …
It was time, for me to take control
To complete myself too whole
To let go, of a decorated enemy once known
I had to let go, for the bettering of me
I had to keep my head high
For the reminder, that I am free
I did everything, for me
Finally

The Understanding

The best thing that you can do for yourself is to respect yourself. Set standards as to how you believe you deserve to be treated. Learn to see with your mind, and not always your heart. In life there will be difficulties that will test your strength both emotionally and mentally.

It is up to you to know what is deserving of your time. Ultimately you choose how you want to be treated. If you carry yourself, with a lacking love, people will treat you as such. Always carry yourself, as if you truly love yourself, and make it known that you are willing to put yourself first.

Know that any form of abuse should never be tolerated. Whether it be mental or physical. You were not born into this life, to be abused. Know when to walk away, in circumstances that make you feel broken. You hold the power and key to your life. It is crucial to be surrounded by those who value the person you are in wholeness.

Avoid disrespecting yourself and be open to having the capability to set boundaries. Know that the people and actions that you tolerate are aspects of how you truly feel about yourself. Have the courage to choose yourself, even if it feels challenging. Understand that conquering a fear is the root of self-elevation.

Held Inside

She got tired of asking why
Like why …
Do wounds re open …
Causing my love life suicide
Why…
Do my tears not bring me relief
But only remind me of the grief
Why…
Why do I objectify myself in a sexual sense
Why …
Why do I not see my worth beyond traumatic intimacy
I still cry in my dreams
I run away , from my fears
Carrying a weight of all of my tears
Worried about my self-esteem ,

As I am unable to see the inner me
Blind to the fact , that apart of the inner me …
Is indeed an enemy
She's seen things , she couldn't control
Haunting memories that she witness unfold
In truth …I think she's bold
Her heart never turned too cold , instead it was her youth …
That she felt life owed
Her innocence , that once had been stole
A love manipulated through the action of taking advantage
She now burns flames , to fight through the damage
They all asked why …
But never not once …
Knew what she held inside …

The Understanding

It is crucial to understand the importance of letting go of pain. Holding traumatic emotions within, indeed does more damage than healing. Trust, the answers you seek will come when your mind is at peace. If you have experienced abuse in any form, know it is not the defining of you. Self-worth derives from the development of love within. You must love yourself, more than the pain.

Being honest with yourself is one of the greatest deeds you can do for yourself. Avoid running away from your problems, face the reality of what bothers you inside. Do not allow any form of trauma to stray you away from being the truth of who you are inside. Be committed to letting go of anything that no longer serves you. Express yourself to release, and never allow the past of anything to hold you back.

Wonders in the Cold

You keep your eyes half closed
Lacking love, in the coldest of snows
You bundle up tightly
Holding onto memories that felt warming
Slightly …
You walk on the clouds
With your mind out of your control
And I wonder …
Beyond your escapism, what makes you feel whole?
I see you …
You wonder the journey of life alone
A family, that is long gone
No home …to claim as your own
They call you the toxins of the worlds garden
Unaware that from peace and sanity
You have long departed …
Craving intimacy beyond the physics of sexuality
You yearn for the hug that embraces your abandoned energy
I see you …
And no…
You're not my enemy
You are a friend to me, I pray for
I pray you find better beginnings
And encounter beautiful endings
Someone cares …
I see the heart of your tears
For you…
Darling …I pray for better years

The Understanding

To those who have walked life alone, I want you to know, it gets better. Keep
a spirit that never gives up, no matter how tough life gets. When you think

there is no one that cares, trust there will be an opportunity, when someone cares enough to treat you with love, instead of an enemy.

Understand that family is deeper than blood. Everyone that shares your bloodline is not family. Family is a connection and an everlasting loyalty, that binds a group or pair of people together. Forgive those who lack the knowledge of valuing the meaning of family.

In truth, the world can be cold, no matter how kind you are. It is crucial to build character, and stand on what you believe in. Believe in your faith and become better and stronger than any obstacles that were ever placed in front of you. Know that you can become the person you desire to be, leave the past behind. Appreciate the present and become the future you want. Even when others stop believing, never give up on yourself. Always, keep pushing.

Green Snakes

When your hands caressed her hips
I looked within for a search of bliss
As your lips, turned to her kiss
I realized it was myself that I missed
When you looked into her eyes
I could feel my conscious, hinting at lies
As you slid between her thighs
I looked to the sky, wondering why I wanted to cry
When you penetrated deeply, causing her to scream
Appeared …green snakes in my dream
With every hiss
Was the reminisce of a disloyal kiss
Each slither, was the continuous thrusting, of a broken heart
Her moans became the haunting of ringing in my ears
All along my intuition was clear …
And that's why green snakes appeared
Sneakily, you smiled so frequently
Green, the coded color of betterment
Meaning, my escape would evolve me into a better me

Even when a snake surrounded me
I wrapped myself into the love of my own
And while you still search for a home…
I decided, I'll protect the softness of my soul …

The Understanding

Understand that when someone performs a disloyal act towards you, there is a lacking within them. It is crucial to not lose yourself in the actions of others. Disloyalty is lack of moral honesty within self. Be conscious of the idea that you are not in control of anyone else, but self. Be aware that it is your ego, that is hurt when someone does something disloyal to you. Meaning, your ego, wants to harbor the pain, ask questions, all to create an anger and sadness within. The consciousness strictly aims to accept reality. With any situation, whether the outcome be good or bad, learn to accept life for what it is. Acceptance is key to becoming aware of what deserves your energy, and what doesn't.

Know that forgiveness is also a form of acceptance, but even more a great deal of peace with a situation. Do not allow someone to take advantage of you. Accept the truth, move on, and forgive. Forgive their actions, for the sake of peace, and appreciation for the present moment. As you forgive, forgive yourself. Forgiving yourself means not to blame yourself, or to allow the ego to fall victim to other's decisions. Know that the toughest days are the ones that will bring the most character and inner strength. Forgive yourself and others for the continuous growth of self.

What's Enough?
You always …
Always
felt like you weren't enough
Through the depth of your heart

Down to the scarring blood
That flowed through the veins of whispers
Once he told you, you were nothing
Your mother, could not mirror self-love
Simply because
She did not who she was
Family became the enemy of ghost
You left behind a past, that created your DNA
Genetics that caused of you pain
Who do you call, to release all your pain?
You've always felt like you weren't enough
They all agreed …
So, in your thoughts …you proceed
Your head is heavy
Your heart is storming
With the rising aftermath of the drowning of opinions …
Your soul is reviving itself form toxic spirits
That yearn to feed your thoughts of negativity
Soon, you realize you became the enemy
Of your inner me …
They told you weren't enough …
Though indeed…
You only became not enough …
For yourself …

The Understanding

The opinion you have of yourself is the only opinion that will ever truly matter. If you think of yourself highly, then it will show in the presentation of yourself. If you are someone that grew up around people who made you feel like you weren't enough, it is up to you to fulfill what you once lacked.

It can be tough growing up in surroundings that never told you how beautiful you were, how proud of you they were, or just simply that they loved you.

Know that people's actions and habits are reflections of how they feel inside. Feeling like you are truly enough for yourself is a goal worth striving for.

Understand that attempting to be enough, for those who are aren't content with themselves, is a lifelong run. You cannot seek validation from others to validate your self-worth; you will almost always be disappointed every time. Know that your self-value comes from within. Materialistic items will not fulfill the emptiness inside. Fill your voids, with the love of yourself, and truly know that you are enough.

Chapter 4

Tears...Are

Faded Smile

What makes your smile fade away

Does reality hit you …

With dismay
Does the truth ... of your heartaches
Close the lips of your perfection?
Why do you smile for not too long?
Are you afraid of what could come?
Fearing obstacles, that you have only made possible
Your smile can only be created by energy,
Of the choices you decide…
Be the reason your smile purely shines through
Surround yourself
With those who create a beautiful view
All…
For your smile to blissfully shine through …

The Understanding

Some days we have those days, when it seems that a smile is harder to find than a frown. It's those days, when the whole room feels gloomy, eyes feel heavy, but there are no tears to pour. It's the moments when every single regret hits you all at once. When each second feels like you are running, from something that you are unable to face and conquer. These days, a smile is hard to find. However, even on those days when it feels hard to smile, I promise you there is always something to smile for.

On the days, when it seems a smile is hard to find. Breathe. Be aware of your frustration, and every emotion you feel inside. Be conscious of the pattern of your breathing. Soon you will find that if you are in a panic or angry mood, your breathing may be in a rapid state, making it hard to think clearly. However, when you begin to pace your breaths, you will notice that it is okay to relax.

When you are conscious of your breathing, you will be able to control your mood and mentality much better. You'll notice that you are in the moment, and the best solution to a conflict is to find a solution that will not negatively impact your future. Logical decisions help to ease the regret of making decisions while being emotional. Never let anyone or anything allow your smile to fade away for too long, simply smile more and breathe.

Past Storm

The sound becomes faded
Only the murmuring of people becomes the tune
Air becomes hazy and smoky, layered in grief
Soon, you are unable to see
You become blinded from the beauty of reality
Only pessimistic ideals take over your mentality of society …
Your heart pumps in eruption
As your chest feels it is preparing to detonate
Doubts and worry, become the fluid within your veins
Deep breath…as in life, you are trying to maintain
There is an overwhelming production within your brain
Lingering pain, manipulating you into the thought …
That you are insane
Though in truth …
You are not the roots, of what you've been through

Embrace the inner fears and tears
The haunting of emotions that you proceed to control …
Understand…there is power in a flower that simply blooms …
Life is not the defining of a second
It is the awareness and comprehension of the present …
Prioritize the growth of your mentality
Release …truly, the dust of anxiety

The Understanding

It is crucial, for your mind, to be a clean and warm space for you to presently be. If your mind is chaotic, that causes negative emotions to flow through body, be patient with yourself. Be patient with yourself, take the time to question your thoughts and feelings.

Learn what triggers unwanted feelings. Anxiety is never a good feeling; it can sometimes make it feel as if you are going to explode. Know that there are many people who suffer from anxiety, you are not alone, and you should always prioritize your health.

On those days, when you feel anxiety, slow down and breathe. Inhale and exhale… Remind yourself that you are worthy of patience. Analyze your thoughts, take the time to learn your thought process, to manipulate your mentality into being anything you want it to be. Become the controller of your thoughts and avoid letting the past haunt you. Issues within only seep deeper, they never go away.

Deal with hard truths that reside within and know that not being okay is okay. We are all human. We will most likely all have days when we are not happy, and that's okay. Live in the moment and appreciate the day for the present of your existence. Even on the days when life feels overwhelming, know that you are alive for a reason, never let this mentality fade away.

Understood Forgiveness

I yearn to be understood
Rather than judged
To be embraced with trust
Rather than glanced with eyes of disgust
To be told …
That it wasn't my fault
That my actions were traumatized taught
To no longer be afraid
Of what they might say …
To simply do things my own way…
I yearn to be understood
Like the cries and broken hearts in the hood
I don't want to be judged
Like the mother who did it for her kids…
I want to be hugged
With the essence of feeling enough
To know that my worth
Has not degraded to dirt
To truly feel that my value
Is the accountability of love given to my self
I yearn to be understood …
Viewed beyond physical
For my soul, that is light
My human aura will shine even in darkness
I am human, just like you
Quality not calculated from what I've been through…
My love is deep
My soul is complete
Enamored in a purpose
Please…
See me, for me

The Understanding

Forgive those who have hurt you, to allow yourself peace. Know that many people only see what you present them. Grow beyond your pain, to allow the most beautiful elements of yourself to shine through. People will see you for you, when you begin to accept and embrace the truth within you. Do not blame yourself for negative actions others have committed towards you.

Avoid attaching your worth and value to the amount of pain you have endured. The maintenance and appreciation of your soul will reflect on the depths of who you are inside. Refrain from allowing yourself to be defined. Always define yourself. Release yourself from being a prisoner in your own mind and look towards your development of self. Someone who has experienced trauma in any form, may at times feel as if they are lost, or unaware of who they are. It is crucial to learn yourself, focus on what brings you excitement, what makes you angry, and what makes you feel whole. These are beneficial concepts that can guide you into becoming your most chosen self.

Mind Carousel

Some days I want those memories to drown…
To the very depth of the ocean …
Where they can no longer be stolen and told
All through mind …
I wish for fire to burn each remembrance
Like a slow burning incense
Leaving a satisfying aroma of relief
For each image to be swept up in this midst of a tornado
Making it impossible, for any recollection to rain throughout my mental
For the feelings not to be as deep as defeat
I yearn for the day when the clouds are the only thing above my head …
When there is no overwhelming of stress
To make me feel I am less
I hope for the sun to shine on the good times
For bad moments to be swept up by the dance of the wind
I pray for bright skies

Where godlike energy is felt beyond
To be grateful for the times, where I can unwind
Where my heart does not feel like it's in a bind
When tears do not mirror the painting in my mind
For silence to not feel so cold and empty
When tranquility represents pure serenity
A time …when my head is not pressured by the weight of perfection
A moment, when I feel I am okay to feel entirely
Just one second …
When I can accept
Of what's inside of me …

The Understanding

The appreciation of your bad days will be an extra delight to your good days. When you reflect on the moments, when you wanted to escape the present …you will realize that there are better tomorrows. Each one of your bad days built the life and person of who you are today. For anyone to truly appreciate every aspect of life, you must accept the good and bad as they are.

Feeling as if your mind is going in circles, and never exceeding to a place that brings you peace, can be frustrating. It is important to break unhealthy habits, that support any mental chaos. Be aware of your thoughts. Replace negative thoughts with positive actions. Know that you are the only person that can truly hold yourself back, so avoid becoming your own enemy. Be kind to yourself when you are not okay and treat yourself as a person you want to protect. Pamper yourself, with love and appreciation, and embrace every obstacle that you conquered.

The Deepest Rose

My apologies
I didn't wait until marriage
Instead
I closed my eyes, and became a rose
While I forced opened my legs

Hoping to feel meaningful sex
Unaware my expression of pain
Would only lead to regrets …
To the embedded damages inside
I flooded opinions and childhood years
With the confusion of impurity tears …
But I thank God for a blessed mentality
That saved me from acting on impulsive hyper sexuality
And yes, I had days,
When I dwelled on mistakes
Committed actions, that blurred the reflection of my face
But I'm sorry
I thought … I was doing the right thing
Like maybe I was the angel to a lost king
But when you entered me, I didn't feel royalty
I numbed myself for years,
Became invisible to my tears …
Yearning to feel something,
All to evaporate unwanted memories
I put my head into my goals, to avoid suicide
Cutting myself hoping to relive my insides
And I was a frustrated teen
Because damn… I just wanted to be normal
Vision blurred between trauma and hormonal
Quiet thoughts, long walks
Unaware I was a victim
And that your actions were, indeed, not my fault
Though unaware …I questioned every aspect of me
I created illusions to escape into the deepest of dreams
Searching for the freedom of me …
Hoping for the slightest relief
From the heart that I pour …
I became my own level of mature
In acceptance, I closed wounds that were torn
In truth …it was myself I had to explore
To know that I am more …

Beyond traumas that I once mourned
Each aspect of my life
Is the completion of my soul …even more
I'm not sorry,
And to you …
Do not feel sorry
Trust …it was all a part of the journey

Chapter 5
Tears Released

Flower To God

I wonder …

Am I a flower to God?
Is my presence just as beautiful in his garden
Are my tears the watering of unreached wisdom
Yes…I know he sees me
He keeps me breathing, for a reason
Embedded in my soul is purpose
I walk gracefully and thankfully on earth's surface
The sun shines, reminding me to smile
I am a flower to God
He kisses me with moments, to embrace life as it is
I hear the songs of the water, as the waves crash
Each harmony tells me …to relax
You surround me with messages and blessings
When I feel I am less than …
You made flowers …
To flourish, to blossom
…All in a captivating expression
You made me a flower in your garden …
Allowing my essence to be closer to you …
Rather than apart
I Thank you for my heart, my soul,
And the flower that you've grown
Through a soul …you make me whole

The Understanding

We are all flowers of the most high, meaning we should love and treat ourselves as such. Know that every tear shed is all part of the journey. Every day, we are presented with new wisdom, though it is up to us to receive it. If you believe in the concept of destiny, then mistakes are destined for you to complete and fulfill your life and soul. Know that every day experienced is an experience of purpose. You are meant to be here. If you want to talk to the most high, use the voice of prayer. If you want the most high to speak to you, learn to meditate. At times, when our mind is chasing answers, typically we will not be given the answers we seek. The answers you seek will come to you in a state of peace. Allow yourself to see the spiritual beauty you have been blessed with. Imagine your favorite flower. Imagine the most high specifically picking your favorite flower, writing your name on it, and placing it in his spiritual garden. You are beautiful, beyond physical appearance. Beyond a face, there is a soul, something that you should always value and maintain in beauty.

Seen and Embraced

Darling.
I want you to be seen
For that you never get lost in between
To never allow questioning of your worth
To know, that your presence is true royalty on earth
Darling
I want you to know …
It is okay to be you …
Vulnerability is the key to your self-expression
I want you to know …
That being "tough" as your defense mechanism …
Is never as strong …as your god given, natural intuition
See yourself, in a present and futuristic vision
Never dwell on yesterdays,
Always become the betterment of a new day
Know that your uniqueness is beyond a face
Unique …is the warmth in the soul you keep
Understand…that to compete
There is no need
We were all made …to be our own free
Darling …
Become the goals, you are destined to achieve
Fall in love with the idea of complete …
You are completely, you
Alive in the essence, that you appreciate the present
Be the happiness, that caters to your soul
Darling …you are already whole

Trust me…they see you
The god within knows …
Simply …
It is up to you
To know…
To see…
To be …
To embrace
You …

The Understanding

Have you ever felt invisible? Especially when you were hurting inside. Why did the coldest of days feel longer.? The embracing of a hug was nonexistent. You may have even questioned if genuine love even existed. You wanted to be understood, but unable to begin to express the frustration and sadness that dwelled within. You yearned for the affection of others, but unaware of how to let your guard down, to receive it. You became comfortable being alone, in your own solitude.

Never look for someone to complete you. Even when you feel you are "broken", this is the experience of being unable to release pain from the mind and spirit. Learn to be comfortable being you, even when you are not okay. Know that happiness is never a competition. With happiness comes acceptance of life and self. Release yourself, from the past, and become your own freedom. Truly embrace what makes you unique, instead of what makes you weak.

Soul Melodies of Art

I decided that art is a spirit

With peace …you can feel it
Ears of wisdom…you can hear it
Relax … through the soul, there's healing
Let serene Melodies free depressive mentalities
While each soft brush of paint,
Releases the struggles, you overthink
Allow the poetic words
To fulfill you with an adrenaline burst …
Truly understand …
You belong on this earth, with beautiful reasoning for your birth
The spirit speaks to you
It enters you …
When you allow the God within through
Embrace the ability and power of creation
Uncover your light, through meditation
Art is a spirit …of true creation
Know that energy
Are the depths of what you make it …
Free yourself naked
Give yourself a way to idealistic freedom
Truly …you'll discover
The seed of wisdom, you've always needed
Love with eternity, through the soul
Art is the embracing of all creations, unknown
Creating familiarity with souls, who know

The Understanding

Art is a beautiful form of expression. It is the voice of the soul, and the freedom of the mind. It is the ability to create. What you feel. On the days when you feel imprisoned in the mind, do something that makes you feel alive. Yes, it can be art, though if not; what makes you feel alive? Take the time to appreciate and explore what excites you about life.

As humans, we all need an outlet. An outlet allows us the ability to step outside a frame. A frame, of pleasing others, and a frame of feeling exhausted. Finding healthy habits to cope with stress is crucial for the mind and heart. You are a soul with purpose, explore it. Give yourself a chance to become yourself to the greatest extent. Live your life, for you. Live to be alive, not to only survive. You are here for an experience, embrace it.

The Glimpse of Life

Life doesn't always taste like …the sweetness of an orange
It doesn't always feel like a warm relaxation
Life doesn't always have the satisfaction of good sarcasm
The sound is sometimes …
A melody you can hardly comprehend or fathom
Sometimes …
Life can be the taste of the most bitter lemon that burns …
The smell of fear, that leaves an unwanted scent
Life can feel volcanic, leaving your mind in a state of eruption
Life is the soul of all experiences
It can be Beautiful…as the sweetest marriage
Or scornful …like the idea of hell
Though life is the reflection of your human prevail
The combining of optimistic and pessimistic journeys
In all…it is worth surviving
Life never gives up…until it's time
Use each day …as an experience to thrive
In the awareness…that you are Indeed
Alive.

The Understanding

Like many valuable experiences in life. Life in general will have its ups and downs. Life can be thought of in the sense of the Law of Polarity. The Law of Polarity derives from the several laws of the universe, it is the idea that everything has an opposite. Meaning in one aspect there is good, and on the other side there is evil. There is love, and on the opposite end there is hate.

However, though there are two opposite ends, you ultimately decide which end you give the most attention towards.

Life is the perspective of experiences. How you view each experience in life will determine the defining and depiction of life. Know that you must become the light that you want to attract in life. The law of attraction is a law of the universe meaning, you are what you attract. If you are an optimistic person, you will most likely be drawn to people who are just as, or even more optimistic than you. If your mind is filled with pessimistic views, and thoughts that break you down, rather than build you up, then you will attract those with the same mindset. We typically attract those along with the same mindset as us, because it is an alignment of frequency. A healthy mind is key to a healthy existence of life.

The Beauty Life

Life is the beauty and color of the deepest hue …
The most…reflective iridescent deepest rainbow
It is the majestic energy of electricity …
Powerful beyond the norm of mental capacity
Life is a force of love
An element of a soul's journey, that remains untouched
It is the breathing of certainty
And the appreciation of the uncertain
Life is the unexpected …perspectives we gain
Within ourselves …
It is the objections, that we voice through our hearts
Life is the unsaid …destiny of a true souls' spark
It is the architecture of a godlike, work of art …
Life is everything …we were once taught
And all the knowledge we've never thought
It is the necessity of the belonging amongst humanity
The deepest feelings of yearning for clarity
Life is the true expression of a light that is destined
Life …

Unique
An essence that could never be duplicated
Indeed …it is the reality that you make it
Life …is the creation of the created

The Healing

Through each experience we encounter in life, they all help and shape us to become who we are today. Be thankful for the ups and downs and know that you are exactly where you are supposed to be in life. If you are unhappy with where you are in life, only you can fix what needs fixing. Avoid relying on others to complete you or bring you peace. You must become everything; you want and truly believe that you deserve it.

Life can be the game that you excel at, or the game that brings you the most stress. Your strength in life depends on the character of your mentality. Be self-aware to show true love and self-value to yourself. Grow in love with yourself, as well as life. Life will not always be a sunny day, but view life from the perspective that there is more to love, than to dislike. Leave the past behind, heal what once hurt you and know that you are better than the pain of what you've been through. Accept and love life, for the journey and experience that it is.

Dear Readers,

The experience of writing, "I Know Why Black Girls Cry", has been a journey of emotions, that has truly assisted and guided me into creating this novel. I have taken experiences, from self, and the analyzation of different traumas that many Black Women have faced. I wrote this novel that not only aims to make many Black Women feel understood, but to heal inner wounds as well. Any Black Woman, who has experienced any hardship in life, at most times she just wants to be heard and understood. I want Black Women to know, there is someone there, who is willing to hear your story, always someone willing, to take the time to observe instead of judge, though you must be the one to truly embrace and love you. My overall message to you is that life can be tough, though do not allow life to overwhelm you. Enjoy the moments in life, even if yesterday was not your best day, and the past still haunts you. You must decide what is truly meaningful to you. The years of life can pass by fast, be aware that your mentality can become your perception of reality. Be sure to take care of your mental health, as a priority, and be there for yourself. Sometimes, you must be the friend you need, you must pick yourself up, and accept the love of yourself in self-awareness. Know that better days are always ahead, keep being beautiful.

Sincerely,
Kashya Molineaux